RHYMES N REASONS

RHYMES N REASONS

*The Lyrical Expressions of
Bob Marks*

by

BOB MARKS

Copyright © 2019, Bob Marks

All rights reserved. Printed in the U.S.A.

No part of this publication may be reproduced
or transmitted in any form or by any means, electronic
or mechanical, including photocopy, recording or any information
storage and retrieval system now known or to be invented,
without permission in writing from the publisher, except
by a reviewer who wishes to quote brief passages in connection
with a review written for inclusion in a magazine,
newspaper or broadcast.

Published in the United States
by eBooks2go, Inc.
1827 Walden Office Square, Suite 260, Schaumburg, IL 60173

ISBN: 978-1-5457-5046-9

Library of Congress Cataloging in Publication

CONTENTS

Authors Note — ix

1. Seventeen Is A Crazy Age — 1
2. Heaven Bound — 2
3. Destination Paradise — 3
4. Young — 4
5. Golden World — 5
6. If We Could Fly — 6
7. Gone With The Wind — 7
8. Too Old — 8
9. Beyond Compare — 9
10. One Step Beyond — 10
11. The Call Of The Wild — 11
12. Point Of No Return — 12
13. Spotlight In Your Dreams — 13
14. A Midsummer Nights Dream — 14
15. By Love Possessed — 15
16. Nighttime — 16
17. The Conquest Of Love — 17
18. She's So Beautiful — 18
19. Midnight Madness — 19

20. Who Will Be The One	20
21. Only Lovers Seem To Know	21
22. Strange Disease	22
23. Something Special	23
24. Untitled	24
25. Where Do We Go From Here	26
26. Love In The Rain	28
27. Just Let Me Dream	29
28. Wheres That Man	30
29. Forever Amber	31
30. Thunderball	32
31. To The Tune Of Camp Grenada	33
32. Cleopatra In The Morning	35
33. Watergate	36
34. Two For The Road	37
35. Once Upon A Miracle	38
36. Say It With Love	39
37. First Love	40
38. My Ex Wife	41
39. Maybe We'll Make It Together	42
40. Pure Summer Love	43
41. Same Time Next Summer	44
42. Stars On A String	45
43. For Now	46

44. When Worlds Collide	47
45. What Did I See	48
46. Strange Things Are Happening	49
47. One Day Of Your Life	50
48. Twisted Thing	51
49. I Want To Have A Fling	53
50. You Stay In My Head	55
51. Deprivation Of Heritage	56
52. How Could You Leave Me Behind	57
53. One Of Us	58
54. One More Rainbow To Chase	60
55. It Was This Way Before	62
56. Really Don't Remember You	64
57. Wild	66
58. Summer Is For The Flesh	68
59. Once Is Not Enough	69
60. It's Better With Someone You Love	71
61. Love Got In The Way	72
62. Better Late Than Never	73
63. Thinking	75
64. Don't Remind Me	77
65. Office Wife	79
66. I Need Some You	81
67. Final Thoughts	83

AUTHORS NOTE

Not sure which famous philosopher theorized that the mass of men were far too busy just earning a living to ever really make any serious money. It might have been Thoreau.

I'd imagine that similar applies to the creators especially those too exhausted from the day's labors to seriously devote significant time to their creative passion until they finally reach the point where they lack the energy to do either.

Unfortunately, far too many do pass on with their music still inside them.

The following is a collection of lyrical expressions over the years some of which have been published and/or set to music, though I've yet to earn a nickel from it.

At this point in time, with creative energy waning from the long and winding road to age 76 (those that know me are well aware that I've seldom had an easy moment along the way. Fortunately some do applaud my accomplishments. Real proud to be a member of the harness racing communicator's Hall Of Fame).

Be that as it may, in my earlier years, I extensively studied how the masters like Cole Porter, Irving Berlin, Richard Rodgers, Alan Jay Lerner, Fredrick Lowe, Stephen Sondheim, and Neil Diamond (yes Neil Diamond) patterned their works in accordance with accepted song patterns of their eras much of which is still in vogue today. There are some modern writers I've noticed like Springsteen Jimmy Webb and Billy Joel who deviated from conventional patterns but that probably just adds to their overall individual genius especially since they also write their own music. Who knows, maybe there's someone out there searching for a specific rhyme or reason and if so, collaboration will be welcomed.

As for me, I'm just a hope chest lyric writer but I'll let you, the reader judge that stuff. Personally I believe that one or two of the original selections listed here had or may still have the makings of being considered standards assuming of course it resonates with a quality singer with the ability to interpret and enunciate the emotions therein.

Thus I've compartmentalized this work into three stages. The early stage comprised of stuff I wrote in my teens and early 20's. The influences there were the lively new doo wop and Rock n roll music I was hearing in association with the popular stuff, I was familiar with having been exposed to Eddie Fisher, Perry Como, Sinatra, Don Cherry, Doris Day Ella, Sarah Vaughn etc.

The middle range came as I hit those "middle years" which actually might be a tad more sophisticated as by that point I was greatly influenced by Neil Diamond and to a degree Bob Dylan though I found it hard at times to apply patterns to his melodies though I loved his words. Diamond's patterns were easier to discern being more conventional to his era.

Then there's the later stuff which might be more conjecture than actuality.

But again, I'll let you decide.

In that Rhymes and Reasons are songs, not poems, I've left them in the accepted patterns necessary to set them to music. There may be some repetition but rare is the song sang in its entirety without repeating verses or choruses especially, what is now considered the chorus. The earlier songs were primarily AABA or ABAC patterns which were the norm back then.

As patterns evolved into the more contemporary verse-chorus mode, I'd suspect that happened because repetition of the chorus allows for more rousing concert finales in which audience might be tempted to sing along.

As a harness horse breeder, I was considered way above average at naming the horses we bred, the reason being that I always felt every horse was born with a name originating from the names of its parents but the key factor became was I good enough to think of it. Often I was but sometimes not.

Similar applies to lyric rhyming. Just about every word other than orange that one might use to end a lyrical line has a rhyme but are we clever enough to think of it. I'm constantly changing words in the lines you'll read as suddenly something popped into my head that made better sense than what was written. I'm told rapper Eminem was a master at incorporating hinge, fringe and singe into the same rhyming meter though I have no confirmation as I've never listened to rap.

Incredibly enough, the next to last line on Something Special popped into my head while I was sitting at Duffy's in Coconut Creek, Florida watching my beloved New York Football Giants self destruct again.

For 40 some odd years, I was dissatisfied with the final A verse in what was an AABA patterned song, though I always liked the melody. And suddenly there it was—simple but perfect. Oh well, "Better Late Than Never!" Hey that's probably the last good lyric I wrote although Office Wife is coming along especially with the just improved chorus.

Your witness my reader!

SEVENTEEN IS A CRAZY AGE

Seventeen is a crazy age
You're too old to do the things you used to do
You're too young to do the things you wanna do
Seventeen is a crazy age

Seventeen is a crazy age
You'll fall in and out of love so very fast
It ain't the first time and it sure won't be the last
Seventeen is a crazy age

Lots of wild anticipation
And sometimes a tear or two
Lots of trial and tribulation
But somehow you get through
You do

Seventeen is a crazy age
Things look murky light will somehow intervene
Lucky that's the way it is when you are seventeen
Seventeen is a crazy age

Inspired by something Ricky Nelson said about being 17. He could have sang this one as it has a good driving ballad beat typical of what was written then

HEAVEN BOUND

Heaven Bound
One kiss from you and I'm heaven bound
Though my feet are still on the ground
Feel like I'm floating on air.

Heaven Bound
Never thought I'd be heaven bound.
My heart's a beating that crazy sound
But I really don't care

Just look what one little kiss can do
You got me yearning burning with love
You enchant me excite me thrill be so much
I'm on cloud nine somewhere above

Heaven bound
You and me baby we're heaven bound
Gonna turn this world upside down
Now that we fell in love

You could dance to this. A simple AABA pattern but that was in vogue back then

DESTINATION PARADISE

When I see the love shining in your eyes
I'm riding high in the sky
Riding high on a satellite
Destination paradise

Say good bye to everyone I know
Off I go and swinging low
Swinging low on a new rainbow
Destination paradise

Whenever you are close to me
It is such a temptation
To hold you tight and never let you go
Wouldn't that be a sensation

Each time you move your luscious lips
Honey drips in double dips
Took a sip and then I flipped
Destination paradise

My guitar teacher said use the word satellite in a lyric so I did. It may have been appropriate back then in the late 50's. Typical AABA up tempo—I was not a very good guitar player.

YOUNG

Young
Destined to become
Those who are among
Natures chosen few

Sweet
Never indiscreet
Each kiss is a receipt
Precious as the dew

Here we stand wonderland
Filled with exotic mystery
Time will tell that this spell
Will linger long as you're with me

Dreams
To build eternally
Will be our recipe
For love forever young

Maybe Paul Anka said something somewhere.
It's more of a syrupy ballad. Simple AABA

GOLDEN WORLD

Golden World
When you're in love you're in a golden world
Never thought your head could spin and whirl
Suddenly you know

Simple schemes
Seem to blossom into splendid dreams
All at once you're acting seventeen
And you got a glow

Your domestic training
You need no more suppress
You know you're entertaining
The chance to answer yes yes yes yes

Golden world
Ain't no denying life is golden girl
The world's an oyster babe and you're the pearl
In your golden world

This can be done fast or slow with two very distinct melodies.
I actually like both versions.

IF WE COULD FLY

If we could fly
Think how happy we could be
We'd see rainbow's ends beyond that bend
Where sky meets sea

We could sail the stardust trail
Buy a condo in the sky
Baby you and I
If we could fly

And we can fly
It's not as hard as it may seem
Never never land is right here at hand
When you can dream

Make it you and me exclusively
No more clouds need pass us by
We'll be riding high
Cause we can fly

Kind of show tooney. Once heard a voice like Doris Day do the first part and she soared the high notes. It has show tune rhythm not rock n roll.

GONE WITH THE WIND

Gone with the wind
That sweeps the plain
The stars grow dim
Here comes the rain

Though you are gone
Love lingers on yet still
Here in my heart your image stays
As must it will

Gone with the wind
Without a trace
Relentless wind
Laughs in my face

But late at night
An appetite still burns
Gone with the wind but somehow wind
Seems to return

Don't know who said it but someone suggested songs should have major titles. I'm sure there's other Gone With The Winds in the great American songbook somewhere.

TOO OLD

Too old you're told
You're much too settled to be bold
They say that when you reach middle age
You can't keep up with the latest rages

Too old they scold
The dreams you peddle have all been sold
You're like a bird with a fractured wing
You won't keep up with what's happening

But you know
You can bubble like champagne
For when there is something ventured
Sometimes there is something gained

Too fit their mold
Just keep your kettle from growing cold
And stay in sight of the pot of gold
You may not ever get that old

BEYOND COMPARE

Beyond compare
The jolt I felt when I first saw you there
The sudden thrill was beyond compare
Like a vintage wine

And do I dare
Run to you or do I only stare
With eyes aglow that only are aware
They've begun to shine

Should I wait
Or should I run to you with heart in hand
Hesitate
Then we may miss out on something grand
And

They say beware
Don't cha let your feet just walk on air
Love it something only two can share
It's beyond compare

Inspired by Paul Vance and Johnny Mathis' Should I Wait. Mr. Mathis could sing this one.

ONE STEP BEYOND

One step beyond
The world that we know
One step beyond
Where warm is the snow

I saw you I kissed you
Enchantment was mine
How long I had missed you
How long I'd been blind

One step beyond
And how hearts can burn
Then you were gone
The meeting adjourned

I'll always been chasing
That one magic wand
To aid in retracing
That one step beyond

Some wonderful song named Magic Garden buried on a Mathis album possibly Stairway To The Stars included the line warm is the snow. I guess I did too. A ballad

THE CALL OF THE WILD

Like a lightning bolt in stormy weather
Like Cleopatra cruising down the Nile
Temptations all around you so when my arms surround you
I respond to the call of the wild

My pulse always raging like an ocean
Yet In your arms I'm helpless as a child.
You got some devil in you the voodoo you continue
When your touch brings the call of the wild

Your eyes two ambers hot as flaming stars
Have lit a fire burning in my heart
I never knew witchcraft could be so heavenly
Till you cast your spell on me

We meet in a rendezvous of our house
Somewhere where love will always be in style
Ain't nothing quite so lovely as hearing that you love me
The sounding of the call of the wild

Jack London wrote The Call Of The Wild. Read it in my teens.
Don't know if the A patterns are precise–They are now. Up tempo

POINT OF NO RETURN

Shy at inception
While the wonders are affirmed
Then it's all acceleration
To the point of no return

Half way to heaven
Little blaze begins to burn
Little storm becomes a cyclone
Near the point of no return

The threshold to love a shaky plateau
Cross it or just pass it by
Decision you make to stop or to go
Is one you must live with for life

Sooner or later
When there's no place left to turn
When the heart runs out of options
That's the point of no return.

Kind of a driving ballad that was in vogue back then when couples might grind a bit on the dance floor.

SPOTLIGHT IN YOUR DREAMS

The spotlight in your dreams
A stage where love light beams

Let my reflection shine
With things you have in mind
When you're lost in reverie

Your hair so fair it gleams
A halo filled with dreams

When sleepy heads slip down
They should be wearing crowns
As princesses mature into queens
My heart and I
How breathlessly we'll sigh
Until we're certain our love you'll keep
In the spotlight in your dreams

Inspired by Cole Porter's Easy To Love, So Nice To Come Home to in which his patterns were ABAC

A MIDSUMMER NIGHTS DREAM

A midsummer night's dream
Imagination extreme

Right there you were
So warm so bold
A mood you stirred
A heart you stole

A midsummer night's dream
Exhilaration supreme

It lingers on
Though summer's gone
But when there's grass glowing green
Somehow again
Gonna love love love and then
Fulfill that midsummer night's dream

Written at the same time as Spotlight for the same reasons though I borrowed the title from the classic Shakespeare novel

BY LOVE POSSESSED

By Love Possessed by love obsessed
Emotionally it's tearing me apart
By you caressed by passion blessed
Just what have you been doing to my heart

First sleepless nights
Then wildest dreams
Could this be right
Strange as it seems

By love possessed I must confess
It's not too hard enduring all this pain
It's come to be pure normalcy
As long as I'm imprisoned in your chains

I'll sail each crest
From sigh to sigh
By love possessed
By you am I

Sang this for Jerry Wechsler of Atlantic records as a ballad, when I can't sing and was super nervous. Should have done it up tempo as the melody works better that way.

NIGHTTIME

Nighttime and you
Stardust in view
Glistening in your eyes

Nighttime is only what you make it
Let's love and have the world pass us by
Passion is ours and we can take it
The moment's too real to be denied.

Whispering wind
Whistles within
Echoing all your sighs

So as we drift along enraptured
Nighttime fades and dawn appears
May we live this moment we've just captured
Year after year after year

Changed this a thousand times to make the B parts identical then went back to the original ABAC

THE CONQUEST OF LOVE

The conquest of love needs only a shove
Then you're plunging into the unknown
But the perils you find can seem rather benign
If the plunge isn't taken alone

It when two pair of eyes happen too synchronize
And lock in on a beckoning call
Then the warning of words can seem rather absurd
As there's nothing to cushion your fall

Such obsession within
The unknowing heart
No depression can dim
That on glowing spark

It's the moment of truth when the uncertain youth
Sees the handwriting clear on that wall
The conquest of love is the fulfillment of
The greatest adventure of all

Wrote the last four lines first then had to build around it. Really think if Mathis or Sinatra sang this it had the makings of a standard.

SHE'S SO BEAUTIFUL

She's so beautiful
Enchanting as a moonlit isle
She's so beautiful
My world revolves around her smile

It's such confusion when an illusion ends
And is there for everyone to see
I can't believe that she
Is really in love with me

Her eyes are beautiful
Some stars pay homage to their shine
And it was beautiful
Sensing different worlds entwine

Explosive chemistry when she kisses me
As her touch intoxicates like wine
She's so beautiful
If only because she's mine

Don't know why but I thought of Johnny Mathis doing this ballad

MIDNIGHT MADNESS

Midnight madness
Happens each new moon
Midnight madness
Passions coming soon

It's really been wonderful
Holding you again
How long will you linger till you
Vanish and then

What stimulation
Induces fantasy
Hallucination
Or just insanity

Midnight madness
Bewitching hour is near
Am I asleep or are you
Really here

We've all had those endless nights and haunting dreams.

WHO WILL BE THE ONE

Who will be the one
Who will love you when you're done
When you're done running around

Who will be the one
The lucky one to call you hon
When the sun's settling down

Never have I been inquisitive
Always left the book on the shelf
Time I took up some initiative
And found out for myself

Who will be the one
For whom all others you will shun
One you'll run to in white gown

Simple little ditty, that Don and Phil might have done.

ONLY LOVERS SEEM TO KNOW

How to dream in between
Crossing streets against the green
Where the rose lies exposed
Only lovers seem to know

Just a trace on a face
Stare so blankly into space
What this pose can disclose
Only lovers seem to know

Only loves know the sign
Cloud nine has no ceiling
Only lovers can define
When a heart is reeling

Starry night precious sight
Eyes that sparkle with delight
How they glow what they show
Only lovers seem to know

Could be done several different ways.

STRANGE DISEASE

I am weak destroyed by your desire
You look at me such wonders you inspire
I got a heart tense as a voltage wire
What is this strange disease called love

I thought you just optical illusion
But you're real to add to my confusion
Then we kissed a marvelous intrusion
What is this strange disease called love

Is it surprising that I feel so ill
Loves outrageously contagious they say
And if an epidemic should break out tonight
I'll throw all my medicine away

Don't stop me now I feel that fever rising
I want to hear what's written in them eyes
This illness is a blessing in disguise

A wonderful disease
Has me shaking in the knees
What is this strange disease called love.

Needs work the A versus didn't match. They do now

SOMETHING SPECIAL

Maybe you're not a ten like centerfold
But you're still the only one I wanna hold
Maybe you'll never be a celebrity
But you'll still be something special to me

Maybe you're not domestic superstar
But I'd rather be with you than in the bar
Maybe it's your individuality
That makes you something special to me

My heart was once all locked up
Now you hold the key
Hope you never lock me out
Loving you is my specialty

Maybe you're not the social butterfly
You're kinda like a drug you just keep me high
Maybe you'll never be all you hope to be
But you'll still be something special to me

Started this in my mid 20's. Revised it a million times, until finally finishing in my mid 70's. Didn't write the next to last line until it popped into my head while watching the New York Giants self destruct on October 22, 2017. And in my humble opinion, it was worth waiting for as that next to last line makes the song.

UNTITLED

Stars at night
Never did shine so bright
Here they are in your eyes
And here they'll stay
Gonna pray

For we've found
A predominately sweet sound
So uncommon to
Those on earth who cannot see
Love is worth eternity
Just you and me

Soft and low
Gonna whisper love you so
Little embers will surely grow
To blazing desire
Can't fight that fire

For in time
Two hearts just gotta entwine
It's inevitable
That we open every door
Stand alone nevermore
Just you and me

The only one where I actually wrote the melody first then added words. Still don't have a title

WHERE DO WE GO FROM HERE

Where
Where do we go from here
Now we've replied we do
Now we've implied we two
Can make it through the years

Where
Where do we go from here
Should these delicious dreams
Merge into vicious schemes
Festering doubt and fear

If I seem apprehensive
Of what the future brings
Pressures become intensive
Upon exchanging rings

So if I may question dear
As you remove your clothes
As you improve your pose
Where do we go from here

I gotta know
Where do we go
From here

Don't all newlyweds ask this question after the first major disagreement?

LOVE IN THE RAIN

Love in the rain
Is never tame
It has to be completely free and wild

Incessant rain
Tastes like champagne
Soaking wet our two hearts met in style

Love in the rain
May be insane
Just like torrential showering of stars

Love in the rain
No more a flame
Just memories gently burning in my heart

Should have a bridge and maybe a chorus.
Maybe I'll get around to it

JUST LET ME DREAM

Just let me dream dream
That I'm am here with you
And that you're holding me
The way you always do

Each night I explore
A world of fantasy
With the co star
Of my reverie

See you standing there
Tempting lips of wine'
Moonlit lace for hair
Tender eyes that shine

I know that I will love
Being loved by you
So let me dream
Till that dream comes true

Jazzy. Not Rock. . . Frank Sinatra type inspired by Rodgers & Hammerstein's I Have Dreamed

WHERES THAT MAN

Where's that man
Wasn't he just beside me
Where's that man
Buried so deep inside me

How did he let himself forget him self
Oblivious to his wealth of self
How did he happen to unwrap into
This frivolous brew untapped on cue

Where's that man
Wasn't he born when I was
Where's that man
Stalking the dawn of my dusk

Can his retrace his step replace his step
Somehow someway re-embrace his step
Or would he re-compete half obsolete
Adrift in waters of self deceit

Where's that man
Hot as a pot of tea is
I'm that man
Why am I not as he is

Wrote this languishing in Florida in the late 60's prior to being lured back to New York by Most Happy Fella. The horse not the play!

FOREVER AMBER

Forever amber forever gold
Always remember all you are told
When moment rises spontaneously
It just disguises that rain you must see

Forever amber visions they mold
Intrepid gambler not sure and not sold
When those surprises appear in midstream
It mobilizes that recycled dream

Destined to wander
In quest of that star
Just over yonder
So near yet so far

Forever amber highways unfold
Imperfect rambler bypassing toll
When moment matters just grasp it right then
Forever amber but never again

Somewhat autobiographical Mobilizes Energizes.
Which word is better?

THUNDERBALL

Kingston Jamaica
So wonderfully enthralled
Subconsciously fearing the worst
The curse of thunderball

Go undercover
Uncover one and all
Try to penetrate those eyes
Disguised as thunderball

Lightning the other accomplice of rain
Forcing the heart to incite
Thunder is just the sounding of flame
For a year for a week for a night

Swim barracuda
It's written on the wall
The only way to beat the heat
Is greet your thunderball

Where's Tom Jones when I need him? This could have been the theme for the Bond movie.

TO THE TUNE OF CAMP GRENADA

Hello Mother Archie Bonkers
Here I am at the track at Yonkers
In the first I bet a winner
But at one to two I can't win back my dinner

In the second bet a driver
Should have tested his saliva
No his driving wasn't shabby
It was reminiscent of a New York cabby

Bail me out oh Herve Filion bail me out
If I hear another tout offering a tip
I'll fatten up his lip

In the fifth I bet a mudder
Not you momma but I shoulda
For you see he started breaking
Momma you move faster when a cake you're baking

Take me home oh where's the bus to take me home
I gotta try and float a loan come back tomorrow night
I know I'll do alright

Hey looka me I'm now a railbird
One more loss I'll be a jailbird
Hey this horse looks in fine fettle
But I wish his sulky came equipped with pedals.

Allan Sherman forgive me for borrowing your melody

CLEOPATRA IN THE MORNING

Cleopatra in the morning
Looks just like the average girl
Her face hidden by a mudpack
Her hair a mess of stringy curl

Cleopatra in the morning
Just look at those bloodshot eyes
Her glare is frightening the mirror
The sun hesitant to rise

Queen Cleopatra goddess of the Nile
Has each and every man worshipping her smile
But these lovesick suitors are in for quite a shock
If they look her up when the sun comes up
Her face could stop a clock

Cleopatra in the morning
Caesar rushed back home to Rome
He then left word to his replacement
Hey Marc now you're on your own

Work to do here

WATERGATE

Watergate wallowing in Watergate
Guess who's got the four to eight
Bugging shift tonight

Where ever you go Watergate will follow
We'll wallow
In the things you've done

In the white house
Guess we've got the right louse
Guess whose light we might douse
Nixon is the one

Borrowed the tune from Soldier Boy, written before he resigned.

TWO FOR THE ROAD

Two for the road
Two ala mode
Two share one load
Two for the road

Two hearts decide
Too take one ride
Nowhere to hide
Too stop the slide

And so the road may wind
Curving as it goes
Serving to remind it grows
And so the road behind
Worth the highs and lows
Further to define what shows

Two hearts as one
Two hearts one sun
Too melt each snow
Two for the road

Loved the movie. Audrey Hepburn was absolutely delicious.

ONCE UPON A MIRACLE

Once upon a miracle
The world began to shine
A case of sparkling wine
A shower of champagne
Is it a miracle or only rain

Once the world's hysterical
So hard to illustrate
What will intoxicate
when you ain't touched a drop
Buckets of miracles make hearts flip flop

Your schedule so meticulous
So carefully arranged
imperceptibly seems ridiculous
As things somehow have changed

Once upon a miracle
In just one moments worth
Your life right here on earth
Clearly revolves upon
That lyrical miracle you're leaning on

Always wanted to write a love song and never use the word love

SAY IT WITH LOVE

Say it with love
While your devotion grows
Let your emotion show
Just let the ocean flow
Say it with love

Say it with love
If you are serious
And she's delirious
Don't be mysterious
Say it with love

Come on convey it
Ignite some fire
And she'll display it
If you inspire some secret wires

Say it with love
With just a ring or two
Her sighs must sing to you
See how she'll cling to you
Say it with love

Buddy Greco or Buble would do this justice

FIRST LOVE

We met on a night of tropical splendor
Granted the rite of passage to blend
With only the light that passion can render
Two hearts can ignite and quickly ascend

Behind unlocked doors lie treasures inviting
For what lies in store there is no defense
Temptation implores this is so exciting
Strangers no more we end the suspense

As bodies consented we soon apprehended
Thrills that cannot be replaced
We willingly captured each forbidden rapture
While stars seemed to shoot into space

First love will remain always remembered
Though love unrestrained soon reach an end
Extinguish the flames but never the embers
And dare we complain if it kindles again.

Inspired by Begin The Beguine maybe Mr. Porter's all time best.

MY EX WIFE

Here we are remarried now
Better off than we were back then
Why succumb to curiosity
And try to see if we could be again

I just made love to my ex wife
I just touched base with my ex life
All the old terrain was familiar game
Like a touch of flame but without the pain

Once we were so much in love
But then good love just turned to hate
If we sample an erotic treat
Will our present ties disintegrate

I just made love to my ex wife
I just touched base with my ex life
All the old terrain was familiar game
Like a touch of flame but without the pain

Hey Barry Manilow you could have done this but does it need a bridge as the chorus will be repeated two or three times.

MAYBE WE'LL MAKE IT TOGETHER

Maybe we'll make it together
Show them that losers can win
Maybe we'll make it together
Though it's abused we have been

Maybe we'll rebuild our two shattered lives
Maybe we'll refill some will to survive
Maybe we'll remove those traumatic times
From no longer tormented minds
Maybe we'll make it together

Maybe we'll make it together
Show them just where they were wrong
Maybe we'll make it together
Knowing just where we belong

Maybe we'll rebuild our two shattered lives
Maybe we'll refill some will to survive
Maybe we'll remove those traumatic times
From no longer tormented minds
Maybe we'll make it together

This one too Barry. Your style. Chorus repeated three times.

PURE SUMMER LOVE

New season of
Pure pure summer love
One time each year you can live a year
Time to love enough to last all year

New season of
Pure pure summer love
One time your turf is sun sand and surf
Ride that wave of life for all it's worth

And in July it starts incubating
Flavored by some festive atmosphere
Into August it's accentuating
Though the specter of September is clear

New season of
Pure pure summer love
From beach to bed you will hear it said
Just how summer love is really for the head
Pure summer love
Pure summer love
Pure summer love

We've all said goodbye in September

SAME TIME NEXT SUMMER

Same time next summer
Same time next year
You know that winter sure is a bummer
When your way of life ain't clear

Hey nothing can compare with sultry summer air
When every boulevard seems like a county fair
Same time next summer
Same time next year

Same time next summer
Same time next year
You beat to a tedious drummer
When the life you love ain't here

Can't wait to be with you in summer rendezvous
When summer sun warms skin there's catching up to do
Same time next summer
Same time next year

And you never talk about what happens in between summers

STARS ON A STRING

I'll bring you stars on a string
Rainbows and things
That makes your heart go
Ring a ding ding

I'll bring you moonbeams in June
Flowers in bloom
Emotion geared to
Shake up a room

And we'll be riding high I know
Sidestepping every cloud
Dreams providing after glow
Having all that life allows

And with an intimate swing
To me you'll cling
Making memories
On feet with wings

And what could be more worth
Remembering
Than your eyes aglow
Like stars on a string

For you Mr. Buble

FOR NOW

For now
I will love you for now
I will love you and how
I might even be true

For you
Move a mountain for you
You're my fountain of youth
You keep pulling me through

Disperse all thoughts of tomorrow
Tomorrow is ages away
Rehearse just thoughts we can borrow
Let's turn life's pages today

In case
Things fall right into place
We'll be right in the race
for the future is now

Kinda like Nice And Easy similar tempo

WHEN WORLDS COLLIDE

When two worlds collide
Breaching incumbent tide
Love overrides
Declaring dividends

I saw one sun and one star
One moon and two hearts
All coincide
When two worlds collide
What was before transcends

When two worlds collide
Reaching that core inside
With oversight
There may be fenders bent

I felt some joy and some strife
A fork and a knife
Intensified
When two worlds collide
What was before must end

Published as a poem in a book of pure poetry but I hear a jazzy beat with horns.

WHAT DID I SEE

Reaching peaks of passions grandeur
Sailing crests on lovers waves
Immersed in you I saw the answers
Lurking in that glow we made
Glow we made

What did I see in you last night that I don't see today
Was there a me and you last night or was it just some grandstand play
What was I free to do last night inspiring such applause
I know what I saw in you last night too bad we're so off course

In the process of performing
Soothing scars you cannot see
Yet in the sober light of morning
Best we freshen separately
Separately

What did I see in you last night that I don't see today
Was there a me and you last night or was it just some grandstand play
What was I free to do last night inspiring such applause
I know what I saw in you last night too bad we must divorce

Getting into my Neil Diamond inspired stuff

STRANGE THINGS ARE HAPPENING

Just being together I can feel the spark
Two birds of a feather on a chancy lark
Hey good thing the gang's together and it's dark
Strange things are happening tonight.

If I seem flirtatious it's because of you
The moods so delicious right now you are too
You're making me wish I could go home with you
Strange things are happening tonight

We've all known each other so many years it seems
Contemporary couples with rapport
Suddenly there's two of us comparing hopes and dreams
How come we never noticed us before

If I seem suggestive it's not just good wine
You know whose receptive babe and right in line
We'd best be deceptive or we'll blow their minds
Strange things are happening tonight.

Remember it well Sharon do you?

ONE DAY OF YOUR LIFE

One day of your life is all I can ask for
One day of your life is all it should be
Let's make it a day a day like no other
A day that was made for just you and me

One day of your life has been what I've wanted
The moment your eyes showed the need in your heart
Let's make it a day a day of adventure
A day we embrace what never should start

Hey it's just one day
Of course not Sunday
Maybe a Monday or any day
What do you say

One day of your life I might be content with
As long as I'm sure for that day your mine
Let's make it a day a day all consuming'
A day we replay one day at a time.

Just a pipe dream. Never happened though it could have once or twice over the years but then I often fell for what was unreachable.

TWISTED THING

Twisted thing this golden ring
Legalized entrapment of the heart
Twisted thing what's happening
How could we not for see the problem start

How can simple evolution
Trigger such a change in life
When domestic revolution
Happens to a man and wife

Twisted thing is rendering
A happy home into a battle zone
Twisted thing is tempering
Basic fears of living life alone

How can simple evolution
Trigger such a change in life
When domestic revolution
Happens to a man and wife

Twisted thing remembering
how good it was until it got so bad
twisted thing this wondering
if we could still recapture what we had

Think we've all lived this at one time or another and so often evolution is the killer of relationships as we evolve at different times. Thus what you start out with is not necessarily what you end up with. On both sides!

I WANT TO HAVE A FLING

I want to have a fling with you
A hot and heavy thing with you
Forget that talk about changing life
It's such a hassle rearranging life
I want to have a fling with you
A hot and heavy thing with you

I want to be in touch with you
I could be so much with you
Forget that talk about forever more
You make commitment and it's never more
I want to be in touch with you
I could be so much with you

Don't know where your head is
Or if if you'd agree
That you and me in bed is
Something that could be
Ecstasy.

I want to have a fling with you
Some hot and heavy ing with you
Forget that talk about wedding rings

Things are better when they come in flings
Just want to have a fling with you
A hot and heavy thing with you

Old fashioned lust

YOU STAY IN MY HEAD

You stay in my head
When you linger
Linger longer than you should
Longer lingering is good
It can fill the void

About you I'll dream
If you let me
If you let me get some sleep tonight
Got a hunch you'll cuddle twice as tight
Like I'll be annoyed

I've known instigators
In the art of making fever rise
But oh you're creators
Are deserving of some Nobel prize

The best thing of all
Is no leashes
I can be completely free with you
Better still I can be me with you
You stay in my head

Love lines three and four in the third A section but I fear that's the ultimate pipe dream as it's almost impossible to maintain individuality under the coupling circumstances.

DEPRIVATION OF HERITAGE

It took us both together to make those little kids
We were mismatched together and so we hit the skids
I tried to make our breakup be quite civilized
Yet of late you've turned to hate erased me from their lives

While you're depriving me from seeing them
You think you're jiving me with lies you're feeding them
I'm half their heritage that they'll cease to know
From such tender minds you're making trauma flow

You got all that you wanted new husband and new home
You're one big happy family I'm out here alone'
Yet they're still my children a fact that you ignore
You cut me out you can't shut me up I won't take it anymore

Yeah you're depriving me from seeing them
You think you're jiving me with lies you're feeding them
I'm half their heritage that they'll cease to know
From such tender minds you're making trauma flow

Now you know what the kids really feel my dear.

HOW COULD YOU LEAVE ME BEHIND

I understand the circumstance that made you change your life
I'm sure you felt much more secure with a different wife
I guess all that you wanted was just some peace of mind
How could you leave me behind

I know new obligations superseded those to me
And that your new relations all assumed that you were free
But yet did you consider how it might affect my mind
How could you leave me behind

How could you not be curious at how I'd come of age
They say I should be furious but how do you stage an unfelt rage
And how do you rage at an unread page

No use rehashing what is done what about here and now
We're face to face we're one on one do you stand and bow
Or must we just maintain this game until we're boxed and pined
How could you leave me behind

Hi Pop would have sent you this if I knew you lived that long. Neil Diamond could do this. His kind of Beautiful Noise or Brooklyn Roads beat.

ONE OF US

Sometimes I get to thinking
We could be quite a team
One of us with lots of sense
And one with lots of dreams

Sometimes I get this inkling
Through the business day
Two of us working hard
Together all the way

Is one of us picking up signals the other one doesn't intend
Is one of us mixing up tingles the script don't recommend
Is one of us starting to wonder how we could be we're we free
Is one of us liable to get involved I wonder which one it could be

Sometimes I start reflecting
At the close of day
Two of us separate cars
Heading different ways

Can't escape suspecting
Two hearts share one plight
Heading home to someone wrong
Leaving someone right

Is one of us picking up signals the other one doesn't intend
Is one of us mixing up tingles the script don't recommend
Is one of us starting to wonder how we could be we're we free
Is one of us liable to get involved I wonder which one it could be

Could do a simple bridge and then repeat the chorus

ONE MORE RAINBOW TO CHASE

On the treadmill into those middle years
Got my routine set got my head in gear
Got that crisis planned in its proper place
Got one more rainbow to chase

One more rainbow to chase
One more flame throwing face
One more vision of fantasy
Is it fantasy that we chance to be
Can't let rain go to waste
Got one more rainbow to chase

To offset the creep to complacency
I respect the need for some chase in me
In all likelihood it's a no win race
Just one more rainbow to chase

One more rainbow to chase
One more flame throwing face
One more mission impossible
Is it possible that we're possible
Can't let rain go to waste
Got one more rainbow to chase

You may be over my head
But if I get you in bed
Where inhibitions get shed
We'll equalize
No compromise

One more rainbow to chase
One more flame throwing face
One incision of ecstasy
You sit next to me that's the text I see
Can't let rain go to waste
Got one more rainbow to chase

Set to music they gave it a country feel.
I hear a Diamond feel Mr. Sherry.

IT WAS THIS WAY BEFORE

Catching waves through summer sunsets
One on one with one you just met
Extracting all from momentary thing

Barefoot days windswept evenings
Carefree ways in love believing
Attracting all the words that make me sing

It was this way before
It's gotta be this way once more
Gotta live at last as I dare to dream
At peace with life and with self esteem
It was this way before
It's gotta be this way once more

Had my fill of all that rat race
Drive and strive and stuff that fat face
In fact it's all subverted every spring

Tasted fruit from peak of conquest
Turbulence from constant unrest
Subtract it all and kings will still be kings

It was this way before
It's gotta be this way once more
Gotta live at last as I dare to dream
At peace with life and with self esteem
It was this way before
It's gotta be this way once more.

Inspired by I've Been This Way Before from Serenade And you Mr. Diamond or David Sherry would do this great.

REALLY DON'T REMEMBER YOU

There was laughter there was love
There were dreams that might have been
No more laughter no more love
Just indifference deep within

Looking back on all those years
Who'd believe it's true
I really don't remember you

I can't recall the rise and fall of what it was we were
I know I should be off a wall when memories start to stir
Except there's just that vacancy no scar no residue
I really don't remember you

In the aftermath of love
There are scenes of true remorse
In the aftermath of us
Same old ship just changing course

I wouldn't call them wasted years
Except for one or two
I really don't remember you

I can't recall the rise and fall of what it was we were
I know I should be off a wall when memories start to stir
Except there's just that vacancy no scar no residue
I really don't remember you

Set to music. They got the tune right but need a much better singer

WILD

Wild
That once upon a word
Meaning when absurd
Must become routine

Wild injected into heart
Unsuspecting heart
Feels what can't be seen

Suddenly I'm doing things I never thought I'd do
Suddenly I'm feeling things I forgot I knew
Suddenly delicious dreams surface with each smile
Suddenly it's you and me and all I see is wild

Wild
When old familiar ways
Vanish in the haze
Of seasons sights and sounds

Wild
That once upon a time
Poems even rhyme
For reasons quite profound

Suddenly I'm doing things I never thought I'd do
Suddenly I'm feeling things I forgot I knew
Suddenly delicious dreams surface with each smile
Suddenly it's you and me and all I see is wild

Set to music. I envisioned a ballad they did it up-tempo it works. But I still want the last wild to sound like Mathis' "Wildly" from Cole Porter's masterful I Am In Love from the Rhythms Of Broadway

SUMMER IS FOR THE FLESH

Autumn is for first nighting
It's so exciting designer dressed
But summer oh not summer
You know that summer is for the flesh

Winter's for hibernating
And for reshaping your treasure chest
But summer of not summer
You know that summer is for the flesh

Summer is for carousing and for arousing
What seeps within
Summer is that season when rhyme and reason
Backseat to whim

Springtime it may be ring time
There aftering time conjugal mesh
But summer oh not summer
You know that summer is for the flesh

Set to music. It works. Summer has always been for the flesh at least to me.

ONCE IS NOT ENOUGH

Both uptight the other night
Shedding clothes without the light
Made it right the other night
Just like two birds in frenzied flight

And then retreat back to a normal life
Again discreet someone's husband someone's wife

Once is not enough for me I gotta have you more
Once is not enough for we have so much to explore
Once is not enough to know all that there is to know
Once is better than not at all but after all adds up
It's not enough

Skin on skin they call it sin
That don't change the shape we're in
Wrong to slip but whatta trip
Can't let go once you got the grip

Such a mess figuring how to meet
Get so obsessed watching you across the street

Once is not enough for me I gotta have you more
Once is not enough for we have so much to explore
Once is not enough to know all that there is to know
Once is better than not at all but after all adds up.
It's not enough

Kind of envisioned rock tempo, they heard rock ballad. It works

IT'S BETTER WITH SOMEONE YOU LOVE

It was good for you and good for me
But not as good as it should be you see
It's always better with someone
Someone you love

Don't you fret my pet hey you were great
But since she left its second rate not great
It's always better with someone
Someone you love

You can go through the motions
You can sure indulge yourself
You can even get rather into it
You can really share the wealth

But after all is said and done
It can be good with anyone but hon
It's always better with someone
Someone you love

Set to music though it should soar more at the end.

Really think this lyric has all the makings of a standard. Most will agree it really is better with someone you love

LOVE GOT IN THE WAY

Comfortable compatible
Two bookends on display
Seemingly that perfect pair
Till love got in the way

Physical emotional
The forces interplay
All the vital signs were there
Till love got in the way

And how we gonna justify all that we've become
How we gonna alibi all that has been done
Family ties and apple pies commitment without compromise
Secret lives they may survive those complications that arise
And arise

Agonies and ecstasies
In different shades of grey
Really was one grand affair
Till love got in the way

Set to music with a rock beat. Mr. Diamond made for you or Mr. David Sherry.

Trish us for 13 years. A grand affair until Love just got in the Way

BETTER LATE THAN NEVER

Past the surge of middle age crazy
Downhill slide starts kicking in
On the verge of golden age hazy
Dreams sub side horizons dim

Deep within your eyes I see such sunny skies
As though we had a lifetime ahead
There isn't any time to nurture any wine
Only random harvest instead

Better late than never baby better late than not at all
We don't rate forever baby its last hurrah its curtain call
No it ain't too clever baby who'd have thought we still could fall
Hesitate it's never baby better late than not at all

Once designed to reach for the glories
Energy would set the tone
Now resigned to speeches and stories
Memory has etched in stone

Then you look at me like we were meant to be
Apprehension just fades away
Yesterday is done tomorrow may not come
You and me and we got today

Better late than never baby better late than not at all
We don't rate forever baby its last hurrah its curtain call
No it ain't too clever baby who'd have thought we still could fall
Hesitate it's never baby better late than not at all

Set to music. They got the melody and tempo fine but it needs a better singer

Love this lyric. Wrote it on the beach as I turned 60 still designed to reach for the glories but when I hit the 70's the prophetic resigned to speeches and stories kicked in.

THINKING

Look at us the kids of summer
Were we just two kids of summer
Who toyed with life avoiding strife and chains

Wasn't bad through the ages
Love I had varied stages
Though not like what it was like back then

And I am thinking of you as I lie here in bed
Feeling her body warm next to mine
Thinking I'd rather it were you instead
Thinking it more all the time

Senior prom hair so golden
Flashback with moments stolen
From the past we made it last all night

No more blonde out of fashion
Years have gone not the passion
Felt no rust reliving us that night

And I am thinking of you as I lie here in bed
Feeling her body warm next to mine
Thinking I'd rather it were you instead
Savoring us like good wine

What the hell my belle of summer
Were we too impressed with summer
To see the light and know it might remain

What we ran from long ago we
Recognize was just too cozy
For restless youth in quest of truth's domain

And I am thinking of you as I lie here in bed
Feeling her body warm next to mine
Thinking I'd rather it were you instead
Thinking it more with each time

If you're thinking of me as you lie in your bed
Feeling his body near you not mine
Thinking you'd rather it were me instead
Then maybe we're both out of rhyme
Maybe we'll try it
No more deny it
Maybe we'll try it in time.
Set to music but the tempo and the singer does not do it justice

Neil Diamond September Morn style. Where parts are talked rather than sung

DON'T REMIND ME

Don't remind me
Just how close we came
From changing this game
From flirting to flame

It's behind me
The moment has passed
Attraction may last
Resistance is fast

Tempting thought to fool around
Out of town
Different neighborhood
Maybe maybe we could

Don't remind me
There's so much to lose
They won't be amused
You know they'll accuse

Just in time we
Imposed common sense
Despite those intents
We're no more than friends

And yet they say you might as well
Who's to tell
As long as it feels good
Maybe maybe we should

Simple distraction
Despite that little buzz
Normal reaction
It was just what it was

And yet one night if you are free
And I am free
And there's time to kill
Maybe maybe we will

Took years before I realized it needed a bridge before the final chorus. And there it is. I think it fits.

OFFICE WIFE

They tell me get a life and ditch that office wife
They tell me get a lover of your own
She keeps my office life so free from office strife
From nine to five I never feel alone

Wonder what she's wearing when she's sleeping
If she's wearing anything at all
Are there secrets bedroom eyes are keeping
After hours when those passions call

They tell me get a life and ditch that office wife
They tell me get a lover of your own
She keeps my office life so free from office strife
From nine to five I never feel alone

Wonder how she's dressing for the morning
Will she be suggestive or demure
And if she should brush me without warning
Internal fire is so hard to endure

They tell me get a life and ditch that office wife
They tell me get a lover of your own
She keeps my office life so free from office strife
From nine to five I never feel alone

Wonder how we'll handle the convention
Two of us on business out of town
Separate rooms of course by all intentions
But in the lounge defenses can let down

Repeat the chorus.

Still playing around with this,

I NEED SOME YOU

When the pressures bring out the stress in me
That's when I require so much less of me
To refresh the very best in me
I need some you

I know I can't have you all the time
You got your obligations baby I got mine
Still there's a magic only you supply
Like mixing matching chemicals a constant high   CHORUS
To make it through
I need some you
Indeed I do
Require you
Entire you
On fire you
I need some you

When I lag behind in that daily grind
And I can't get solace from those ties that bind
To realign a somewhat stagnant mind
I need some you

CHORUS

When I'm not in tempo with the latest rage
And I won't absorb another unread page
To ensure I don't fall off that stage
I need some you

CHORUS

It is a work in sluggish progress. But I kind of like it.

FINAL THOUGHTS

I've always believed that as we age we tend to lose that distinct ability to keep our individual personality sides from overlapping. Thus we tend to be the same person rather than the work person, the play person, the political person etc that this ever evolving complex world demands us to be. Still it beats the alternative.

In addition, I hope the words keep coming so I can finish RECYCLED DREAM... Sounds like a good title.

Though your best years are behind you
But before you fade to black
Those best years may define you
But you never get them back

Suddenly you're face to face with your younger self
Suddenly you can't keep pace where is that mental stealth
Suddenly these words that flow seem like recycled theme
Suddenly for all you know you're one recycled dream

And as this stage of life, I guess I am.

www.ingramcontent.com/pod-product-compliance
Lightning Source LLC
Chambersburg PA
CBHW030530080526
44586CB00011B/388